MW01127337

Summary of:
ATOMIC HABITS

An Easy & Proven Way to Build Good Habits
& Break Bad Ones

By James Clear

Summarized by:
RockyHouse Publishing

© 2018

either directly or indirectly.

Respective authors own all copyrights not held by the publisher.

The information herein is offered for informational purposes solely, and is universal as so. The presentation of the information is without contract or any type of guarantee assurance.

The trademarks that are used are without any consent, and the publication of the trademark is without permission or backing by the trademark owner. All trademarks and brands within this book are for clarifying purposes only and are the owned by the owners themselves, not affiliated with this document.

RockyHouse Publishing

Contents

Introduction

My Story

I still remember that day. It was the last day of my high school. We were playing Baseball, my friend took a full swing, and suddenly baseball bat slipped from his hands, and it hit on my face. The bat crushed my nose. I had a broken nose, multiple skull fractures, and two smashed eyes.

I remember many people were staring at me and running for my help. I saw blood spots on my clothes. However, at that time I had no idea how seriously I was injured.

Many people and my teachers helped me, holding me upright. We walked slowly to the nurse's office. After reaching there, a nurse checked me and asked many questions like:

What year is it?

I answered 1998. Actually it was 2002.

Then she asked: who is the president of the United States?

I said Bill Clinton, but the correct answer was George W. Bush.

When the ambulance arrived, I had lost my consciousness. And when I reached the hospital, I stopped breathing. The doctors rushed to provide me oxygen but decided to send me to a larger hospital in Cincinnati. They called for a helicopter to fly me in Cincinnati. My mother also climbed in the helicopter with me. I was still unconscious.

When we landed at the roof of the hospital almost 20 staff of doctors were there and shifted me to the trauma unit. I was not in the condition to bear surgery and was in a coma, so I was placed on a ventilator.

My parents were no new to this place and feelings. They were in this same place ten years before, when my sister was diagnosed with leukemia. She was three years old, and I was five years old at that time. But, after two and a half years of pain, stress, anxiety, chemotherapies, and treatments my sister was recovered and became cancer-free.

While I was in a coma, the hospital staff sent a priest and a social worker to comfort my parents. By chance, it was the same priest who met with them ten years before when my sister was in this hospital. My mother told me later; it was one of the worst nights I have ever had.

Fortunately, Next morning my breathing showed

some good signs, and I gained consciousness. I felt that I had lost my ability to smell. A nurse asked me to blow my nose and sniff apple juice as I started blowing suddenly my left eye pushed outwards. The doctor said my eye would slowly slide to its place, but it will take time.

Finally, One week later I had the appointment for surgery. After this, I was discharged from the hospital. At this time, I was going home with a broken nose, some facial fractures and swelled out left eye.

These months of my recovery were so hard and slow. I felt that my life had stopped. I was seriously facing vision problems. I was in depression. I was attending different physical therapies that helped me to walk straight in a line. It took me eight months to drive my car again.

In months of recovery, I was anxiously waiting to go back to a baseball field. I loved baseball. My dad had also played in a minor league baseball for St. Louis Cardinals. I wanted to play baseball professionally.

When I returned to the baseball, I was not playing well. I was cut from the baseball team and sent to junior varsity. I was playing the baseball since age four, and I had spent so much effort and time on this sport. And now I was put out of the team. I felt humiliated. I cried a lot that day.

I began college at Denison University after two years of my injury. There first time in my life, I discovered the power of small habits.

In Denison, I decided to make a schedule and get my life in order. My classmates stayed up late nights and played video games while I made a habit of good sleep. I went to bed early every night. My peers put their things in a mess while I kept my stuff in order. I kept my place neat and clean. I started lifting weights multiple times per week. I focused on improving my study and getting A's in my First year. These all were little things and my small efforts in return improved my confidence. It gave me the feeling that I had control over my life.

A habit is a routine or behavior that is implemented regularly. I was collecting many small habits every semester. I had developed my sleep habits, eating habits and strength training habits. I was not aware that all of these little things would go to pay me off.

At the end of the sophomore season, I was the captain of my team and was selected for the all-conference team. Six years after my serious incident, I was selected as a top male athlete at Denison

University, and I was rewarded the university's highest academic honor, president's medal. My name was also written in school record books, in eight different categories.

Although I never played baseball professionally when I look back to my life and all those achievements, I feel satisfied and happy. I feel that I had fulfilled my full potential and that is the reason I am writing this book so that it would also help you to reach your full potential in life. No matter how badly you fall, stay positive and stay focused on your life. You will get what you want in life, but you have to be consistent.

My injury was my biggest challenge I could have lost hope and might have stayed desperate. However, I started to fight against every challenge. In fact, we all face challenges and problems in our life. We cannot achieve success and our goals in one night. You have to be consistent with your habits and struggles. At first, all changes may seem small, but in the long run, they all are going to pay off your efforts and struggles.

I had started publishing articles at jamesclear.com in November 2012. I wanted to share my personal experiment of developing habits with people. Every Monday and Thursday I published a new article. By the end of 2013, I got thirty thousand email subscribers. In 2014 my email subscriber list increased by One hundred thousand and in 2015 I finally reached two hundred thousand email subscribers. At this point, I signed a book with Penguin Random House to write this book. I had made many speeches at conferences in the United States and Europe. People asked me how to change their habits? How to build new habits? How to change behaviors? And what is the formula for continuous improvement?

By the time my articles became so much popular, and they began to appear in Times, Entrepreneur and Forbes in 2016. I started my Habits Academy in 2017, and almost ten thousand leaders, managers, and teachers graduated from there.

In this book, I am going to tell you how to build good habits for your lifetime.

So let's begin!

THE FUNDAMENTALS

Why Tiny Changes Make a Big Difference

1

The Surprising Power of Atomic Habits

In 2003, Britain changed the performance director of Professional cycling and hired Dave Brailsford as new. At this time the performance of Professional cyclist of Britain was worst. British riders had won only one gold medal at Olympics since 1908, and in 110 years no British cyclist had won any challenge. Because of their lower performance level, one of the top bike manufacturers in Europe denied selling bikes to them. They were concerned that it might impact their sales when other professionals saw Brits using them.

Brailsford was different from other coaches. He was persistent with a strategy of small margins of improvement in everything.

He applied this concept as, if you improve by one percent in every step that is involved in riding a bike you will see a significant change when you put them together.

Finally, Brailsford and his coaches started observing a small one percent improvement in every step of cycling. He made hundreds of small changes like he fixed up bike seats and made them more comfortable. He rubbed alcohol on tires for firm grip. He made sure during riding; every rider wears electrically heated over shorts to maintain ideal muscle temperature. He asked the riders to use biofeedback sensors to observe how every rider reacted to workout. He tested many different massage gels for fastest muscle recovery. He hired surgeons to teach riders how to clean their hands to overcome cold. He provided the riders comfortable mattress and pillows for their best sleep. He made such kinds of changes to improve the performance of his riders.

Finally, after five years of his efforts, he made the team win 60 percent of gold medals in the Olympic Games of 2008 Beijing. After four years, they made nine Olympic records and seven world records. This year Bradley Wiggins won first British Tour De

France. Next year, Chris Froome won the race and won again in 2015, 2016, 2017.

From 2007 to 2017, British cyclist won 178 world championships, sixty-six Olympic gold medals, and five Tour De France victories.

Now how did it all happen? How did a loser team transform into world champions? They made little changes in their approach that accumulated into spectacular results.

We all focus on one big important moment that will change our life, but we forget about thousands of small moments of improvement in our daily life. We think remarkable results came from great planning and actions. It could be about losing weights, getting A's in exams, establishing a business, winning a trophy or getting to your goals. We put all our focus and efforts on one huge moment of change. We totally ignore our small daily habits of improvement.

How many of us daily improve our life by one percent? In fact, we don't even notice this one percent of improvement in our task or schedule although It can be very helpful in the long run as those small changes accumulate over time. Let me explain you this concept mathematically.

If you start improving your life by one percent every day for one year, you will be thirty-seven times better at the end, but if you get worse in your life every day for one year, you will come down to zero.

Habits are like compound Interest of self-improvement. Money multiplies itself over the time in compound interest similarly your good habits multiply as you repeat them. They are unnoticeable in one day, but over the months these small habits accumulate and gives distinguish outcomes and results. In the long run, you will notice the value of good habits versus the cost of bad ones.

We cannot admire this idea in daily life. For example, if you study hard for three days a week, you are still not a topper. If you go to the gym three times a week, you are still out of shape. If you save money now, you are still not a millionaire. This is one of the reasons we bounce back to our normal routine and breaks our daily improvement schedule because we want quick results. Because of slow transformation, we readily adopt a bad habit. For example, if you do not work on your project today, you may finish it another day. If you do not eat healthy today, your weight does not move much. If you do not save money for today, you will not get poor today. However, when you start doing such behaviors on a daily basis, you will get worse by one percent every day. And every new day will push you away from your success and improvement schedule. Repeating poor decisions and actions will accumulate in the end, and we have to face the consequences of failure.

Our successful destination depends upon our daily habits and success is also a result of daily habits and not once in a lifetime work. In order to get success in life, we have to work on a regular basis, and we cannot gain success by working once or twice on a task. It does not matter whether you are already successful or not what matters is that what are your current habits because they will put you on the success or failure path.

It would help if you focused on your ongoing improvement rather than your current outcome. You should know on which path you are walking. If you were a brilliant student in your last class but are now in a new class, and you are not attempting your daily homework then you are on the wrong path, and if you do not change your study habits, it's not going to end well. Similarly, if you are a millionaire but you spend more than your monthly earnings then you are on the wrong path, and if you do not change your spending behavior soon, you will face difficulty.

We can measure our outcomes through our habits. If we want to measure our net worth, it can be through our financial habits. Weight can be measured through our eating habits. Knowledge can be measured through our learning habits. We get what we do and repeat. A good act rewards us while our bad act will punish us in the end.

We can easily understand where we will be in the future. We just have to follow our curves of small gains and small losses in our daily routine, and we can see how our good and bad choices will pay us in the future when compounded. Are you spending more than you're earning? Are you making it in the gym every week? Are you eating healthy food throughout the whole week? Are you learning new things every day? These little things will help you to know your future.

Good habits make time your friend whereas bad habits make time your enemy. Habits are like a double-edged sword. Bad habits can cut you down while good habits can build you up.

Your habits can compound for you or against you. There are two types of compounding. Positive compounding which is healthy and productive for you and secondly, negative compounding which proves to be unhealthy and unproductive for you. Positive compounding includes productivity compound, knowledge compounds and relationship compounds whereas negative compounding includes stress compounds, negative thought compounds, and outrage compound.

Productivity compound tells us that if we do one extra task in a day, it may count as a small act for that day but it will pay you in your career. Knowledge compound is if we learn one new idea in a day, it will not make you a genius but if you dedicate to learn every day, it will show a remarkable increase in your knowledge. Relationships compound indicates that the behavior of people depends upon the way you treat them. The more you care for others, the more others want to care for you. If you help others, they will also help you back. You can make your network strong by being kind to others.

Stress compound is about being frustrated. Many little things cause stress in our lives, for example, the tension to perform high in exams, the worry of earning, parenting responsibility, high blood pressure or burden of large families these all accumulate in long-term and cause severe health damage. Negative thought compound tells the more you think to yourself that you're worthless and dumb, you get caught by your thoughts. Outrage compound explains that a series of compound aggression and anger will result in massive scale destruction in the future.

Habits do not make any difference until you cross the line of limit. A major change is the result of many small unimportant and unnoticeable moments. Eighty percent of Cancer is undetectable then suddenly it starts taking over the human body in months. Similarly, Bamboo cannot be seen for first five years but it appears when it builds full roots underground then it explodes within six weeks, ninety feet in the air.

It is very difficult to build habits because when people make some small changes in their lives, they want to get instant results but usually fail to see them. Therefore, they stop making any further effort into developing a habit. For example, you think that I have been going to the gym for three weeks so why can't I see any change in my body? This kind of thinking is harmful to you, and at this stage, you will stop struggling for improving habits.

If you are facing problems to build good habits and break bad ones, it is not because you have not enough ability, but it is often because you have not crossed the Plateau of Latent Potential. This behavior is not good if you complain about your problems instead of facing them or complaining about not getting success instead of working hard. When you finally cross the Plateau of Latent Potential people will call it an overnight success.

The best way to get what we want in our life is by setting goals. Either you want to get A's in exams, establishing your business, getting in better shape, worrying less for your future, want to spend time in other countries, these all can be achieved by setting goals.

This is also my way of life. And this is how I achieved all my habits. Many years ago, I started making a goal of each habit and then reached each goal one by one. I set different goals for different purposes that I want to get. I set my goal for the body and weights I wanted to lift in the gym. I set another goal for business I wanted to establish, I set goals for my grades as well. I was successful in getting some goals, but I do fail in some. Soon I felt my outcomes had very little to do with my goals and everything to do with the system which I followed.

Let me first clear you the difference between goals and the system. Goals are the outcomes or upshot that you want to get, and system is the way or process that takes you to your desired outcome.

For example, if you are an entrepreneur, your goal might be to earn a million dollar in your business. Your system is how you hire talented employees, how you maintain your quality of product and run marketing advertisements. If you are a coach, your goal might be to win a trophy. Your system is how you train your players, how you motivate them and supervise their practices.

If you completely forget your goals and focus on your system, you would still be successful. For example, if you are a baseball coach and you forget about your goal and simply focus on what your team practices each day, you will still get the desired results.

The goal is always to get success or win, the only way to win is to work on a daily basis and to improve each day. If you want splendid results, then you should focus on your systems instead of focusing on setting goals. But it does not mean that goals are worthless, goals do help you in getting direction, but the system is the path to walk towards your direction. It would help if you spent more time designing your system and less time thinking about goals.

Here's an interesting thought: The winner and the loser in any game have the same goal.

Every player wants to win a championship, every employee wants to get the job, every student wants to get A, and every businessperson wants to succeed. The goal of every person is not so different from one another, so the winners and the losers have the same goals. The main thing that differentiates a winner from the loser is the whole system that they were following. Their daily habits and continuous improvements over time.

Do you know achieving a goal is only a small change?

We always think to change our outcomes, but we never realize that results are not the main problem. The main issue is in the system that leads us towards low results. So, the main thing we need to change is our system. You will never solve a problem permanently by achieving a goal. We have all heard of the yo-yo dieters who gain all the lost weight back very quickly once they're off their diets. The reason is that they didn't have a proper system to follow for life. If you want to solve your problems permanently, you need to change your system. It would be best if you directed your focus towards your system and you will achieve your goal automatically.

Do you know goals limit your happiness?

Our common thinking about any goal is that, once I reach my goal, I will be happy. In this way, you always put your happiness off till you get to your goal but before reaching your goal, you have to face many milestones. So you have to be happy and enthusiastic whilst you're striving towards your goal as it will provide you with the energy required to get over inevitable obstacles.

If you are facing difficulty in changing your habits then it's not your fault, the main fault is in your system. The word Atomic habits mean little habits that are part of a larger system. Everyone knows that atoms are small building blocks of molecules similarly atomic habits are small building blocks of splendid outcomes.

2

Your Habits Shape Your Identity (& vice versa)

There are three layers of behavior change. The first layer is changing your outcome. This level is connected with changing your results either it is losing weight, winning a trophy or establishing any business. Mostly your goals are related to this challenge.

The second layer is changing your process. This level shows changing your habits and system. And the third layer is changing your identity. In this level, you change your beliefs, your judgments, self-image, and assumptions.

Your habits depend on how you represent your identity. When you get up early each day, you express your identity as an active person. When you read a book regularly, you represent your identity as an active learner. When you keep your room neat and clean, you represent your identity as a sophisticated person. When you go to church every Sunday, you represent your identity as a religious person. You believe in your identity because you have solid evidence for it.

In my school life, I never thought of becoming a writer. I was an average student in writing. At the beginning of my career I wrote articles just two days a week, Monday and Thursday. By the time, as my evidence of writing grew my identity as a writer also grew.

My habit of writing also grew day by day. The process of developing any habit is the process of developing yourself. It is a very slow process, and you start changing day by day. Your habits are the ways to change your identity. If you want to change who you are, you need to change your habits. By developing a new habit and practicing it on a consistent basis, you start trusting yourself, and your self-confidence also boosts.

To achieve mastery, you need to be patient. All big thing in life come from small beginnings. It is little things that show remarkable results. The seed itself is so , but it transforms into a big strong tree over a long period of time.

In order to change yourself you need to acquire new habits, and new habits mean you should have new identities, new identities mean new evidence. If you keep doing the same mistake you have done many times, then it's like you cast your vote every time to the same thing. To bring a change in your life, you need to cast a new vote.

Einstein once said that insanity is doing the same thing over and over and expecting a different result.

You need to do two simple steps. Firstly, decide the person you want to become in life. Secondly, with small wins prove it to yourself.

To become the best version of yourself you need to be persistent in improving your habits, editing your beliefs, improving your identity and increasing the evidence of your new identity.

3

How to Build Better Habits in Four Simple Steps

A psychologist Edward Thorndike, performed an experiment on a cat to understand how habits and behaviors develop. From this experiment, he concluded that, if we repeat an action many times it becomes automatic after some time and turns into a habit.

Whenever you find yourself in a new situation or problem, you have to make a decision. Although you do not know how to solve the problem your brain start taking actions to deal with the problem. In this way, your brain learns to act in a specific manner dealing with this kind of problems. For example, if you are feeling lonely, you might find out that going shopping will make you feel better. Whenever you are mentally upset from long work, you learn that watching a movie will relax you. If you feel unwell taking rest will help you feel better.

These are the solutions you find for your issues. Whenever you feel good with your solution you start applying it again and again, when you feel your solution is not useful, you change your strategy. You try, fail, learn and try again. With practice, you learn more about your behavior and also learn to handle it.

Do you know how habits are formed?

The process of forming a habit is divided into four steps. **Cue** – it activates your brain to start a behavior and to estimate a reward. **Craving** – it is the source and a reason for a change. Without craving for a specific thing, you would not be able to achieve it. **Response** – is the actual act you perform. It depends upon your level of motivation and your dedication attached to a specific task. **Reward – it** is our primary goal of why we perform every habit. It helps us to satisfy and teach us.

These four steps can be divided further into two phases: The Problem Phase and the Solution Phase. Problem Phases includes the cue and cravings, it's when you feel change is required while the solution phase consists of the response and the reward, and it's when you get the desired outcome.

When you want to adopt a good habit, and when you want to break a bad habit you can use these four laws.

How can I make it obvious?

How can I make it attractive?

How can I make it easy?

How can I make it satisfying?

4

The Man Who Didn't Look Right

The human brain is very intelligent. It works all day, takes input or information from our surroundings and then analyzes all the info. Brain also recognizes the behaviors or experiences that repeat themselves again and again.

With practice, you can achieve specific results without thinking about them. We have no idea how much our brain and bodies can do without thinking. Many of your reactions are precise and automatic. For example, you do not tell your heart to pump, your lungs to breathe, your stomach to digest, your brain to think.

One of the important things to notice is that before building and developing new habits, you need to handle your current habits. You may have many good habits, so you might want to keep them for your lifetime. It is more difficult to maintain old habits than to add a new habit. You can do any action once but to do this, again and again, is challenging.

The second important thing is when you find any bad habit in your life, you should eliminate it. Before changing the habit, you must be fully aware of your actions. What are you doing in life and why are you doing this? It gives a solution to this problem.

For this purpose, make a list of all of your habits for a day. Once you write down all the list. Then take a look at each habit and decide if this is a good habit, a bad or a neutral one. If the habit is good write +, if it's a bad habit write -, and if it's neutral write =.

In this way score all of your habits. Ask yourself, is this a good habit? Is it helping me?

The habits scorecard is a simple exercise you can use for awareness.

5

The Best Way to Start a New Habit

The best way to start any new habit is to make a plan beforehand about when and where you're going to perform the habit. That's an easy way to implement a new habit. Two most common cues are time and location. At what time am I doing this work and where am I going next?

You can make your implementation intention as:

When situation X arises, I will give response Y to that situation.

Many studies show that implementation intention is very useful for pushing your goals. It's like writing down the exact time and date of your goal or habits. For example, write down the exact time of your sleep, a specific time for study, eating time, etc. It will help you to stick with your schedule.

Research has proved that when we ask people different implementation intention questions in a survey, their response rate increases.

You should have one thing clear that if you make a specific plan for when and where you will execute a new habit more easily. For example, you think I will eat healthier. But, when? So, if you make a thirty-day diet plan of eating healthy food and also write specific times of eating and what to eat. You will be more likely to achieve your goal of healthy eating.

One big advantage of implementation intention is you do not need to wait for motivation. You have already made a plan the only thing you have to do is to act without thinking of anything else. For example, do I eat healthy today or not? Do I make drawing practice today or not? Do I get up early today or not?

If you do not know how to start your habits, use this strategy:

I will [Behave] at [Time] in [Location]

It will help you in achieving your tiny daily habits without wasting your time.

My favorite strategy is Habit stacking.

Habit staking is a special form of implementation intention. In this concept, you pair your new habit with your current habit. The unique thing with this method is linking your desired behavior with something you are already doing. So it makes it easier to adopt a new habit.

Its formula is:

After [current habit], I will [new habit]

For example.

Meditation: After making my cup of tea in the morning, I will meditate for one minute. Exercise: After reading my book. I will do my work out.

6

Motivation is overrated; Environment Often Matters More

I n this chapter, I am going to teach you how a favorable environment will help you in changing your habits easily.

You can easily redesign your environment according to your new habits so that you can follow them without any problem.

For example, if you want to practice drawing, put your sketchbook in your living room so you can easily approach it.

If you want to work out daily, make a small gym in your house so you can easily do your exercise daily.

If you want to add a habit as part of your life, you first have to add a reminder of that habit in your environment. It's the primary strategy to be attracted towards your new habit. You can create different new routines at different places. You can quickly develop a new habit with a new context. For example, perform a new habit at a new corner of your house, or a new café or new bench of a garden.

If you try to develop a new habit at the place where you already practice another activity, it will be very hard to develop your new habit. For example, if you watch television every night in your bedroom then it will be very challenging to start a habit of sleeping early. Or, if play video games in your living room it will be tough to make a habit of studying there as you will find it difficult to concentrate there.

You can also improve your way of doing any work by changing your environment. If you want to do a big assignment go to the library instead of doing it in your drawing room. If you want to take a break from your daily stressful job, go to the cinema and watch a movie there instead of watching it in your living room.

However, if you cannot create a new environment, try to change the old one. Try out a new place, new corner, and new room in your own house. There should be a clear division between your work life and home life.

7

The Secret to Self-Control

R esearch shows that people who have more self-control are more disciplined in their lives. Self-controlled people are not struggling in their lives. In fact, the secret of self-control is that some people have constructed their lifestyles in such ways that they don't need to panic or lose control of things when they're presented with new situations. They productively manage and show discipline throughout the entire day, and they have good habits and a schedule for doing every task of the day.

By creating a disciplined environment, you will automatically grow self-control. You do not need to be a superhero in order to avoid temptations you simply have to spend less time in a tempted environment. The more you avoid such environments, the more you became good at self-control.

Try to develop good habits. For example, if you make a habit of early sleeping you will avoid late night parties, by doing so, you can make the next day productive by getting up early. I am not telling you to stop enjoying your life but I'm encouraging you to lead a more disciplined life.

Bad habits are tough to change. They are like a chain reaction. Once you do a bad act, you will start doing another bad action in its response.

For example, if you are obese, you eat junk food then you feel bad and to make yourself feel better you eat more garbage. Eventually, you become fatter so you feel worse and then you start eating junk again to get a little dopamine hit. You watch television because you feel like slacking, then you watch more TV because you do not feel active and have low energy.

Researchers call this "cue-induced wanting." Any bad act becomes a cause to repeat a bad habit. You can break a bad habit if you overcome its exposure. For example, if you want to stop drinking just stop going to bars and clubs. If you cannot concentrate on your work just put your phone off. If you spend too much time watching movies, then place your television outside your room.

Remember the law of behavior. Instead of making it visible, just make it invisible. Breaking the cue will break the habit soon.

8

How to Make a Habit Irresistible

The simplest way to make any habit irresistible is by enjoying it when we start to enjoy doing a habit, and it's almost certain that we will perform it over and over again. You can apply the second law of behavior: make it attractive. You can try to add different temptations to make your habit more attractive. For example, if you want to make a habit of daily working out, you can make your habit more interesting by playing your favorite song list during the workout. You can go for a pedicure and can check your emails at the same time.

Temptation bundling is a psychological theory. It says that, If you don't want to do your habit, you will become conditioned to do it if it means you will also be able to do something else that you really enjoy.

You can get splendid results if you combine temptation bundling with habit stacking strategy.

Habit stacking + temptation bundling formula is:

After [Current Habit] I will do [Habit I need]

After [Habit I need], I will [Habit I Want]

For example, if you want to check your Instagram but you need to do exercise.

After I pull my phone, I will do ten pushups. (Need)

After I do my ten pushups, I will check my Instagram. (Want)

This is a very simple strategy; to do what you want you first have to do what you need.

Habits are dopamine-driven feedback. When the dopamine we receive from any habit increases so does our motivation to act. Now, what is dopamine you ask? Dopamine is the main chemical of pleasure that releases in our brain and body. So if our habits are attractive and exciting, we have the urge to do them more because doing them will help release dopamine which gives us pleasure. It is the expectation of reward that persuades us to take action. The higher the expectation, the higher the dopamine.

9

Role of Family & Friends in Shaping your Habits

Who is a genius person? Genius can be anyone who is educated and undergoing careful training. So with the practice of good and effective habits any child could become a genius in any field.

Human beings are social animals. We want to belong with others and be recognized as a respected person in the society. Humans always lived as a tribe. Mostly our habits are shaped by our society, family, and friends. Our preliminary habits are picked up by our parents, family, teachers, and friends. There are also social rules and norms in every society, and people have to act according to their society. So mostly we follow the habits of our culture, religion, and society without thinking.

And, we especially follow the habits of these three groups:

The close: we pick the habits of our close ones without realizing it. We also pick many habits from

33

our environment, our parents and our surroundings. So it's very easy to pick good and bad habits because we are adopting habits without thinking. There is a solid chance that you have had a good as well as a bad company while growing up. So in good company, you will adopt good habits, and in bad company you will adopt bad habits very easily.

In an environment, we keep checking what others are doing and then shape our habits accordingly. It's a smart strategy. However, it has a demerit if you are always looking to pick up the habits of others, they may not align with your goals.

We all want power, authority, recognition, rewards, and medals. We find those behaviors attractive which give us respect, health, wealth and approval in the society. Everyone wants to be the best among all. Therefore, we should be more concerned with the habits of high achievers and successful people. We should adopt the strategies of top performers to be successful like them.

In order to adopt good habits of winners, you can join a group of successful individuals.

10

How to Find & Fix the Causes of your Bad Habits

Y ou should first find the cause of your bad habits and then fix it by applying inversion of the second law of behavior change i.e. make it unattractive. For example, if you are a smoker, educate yourself how smoking is injurious to health. Read a book like Allen Carr's way to stop smoking. This book sets you free from mental disorder, and it teaches you strategies to make your habit of smoking unattractive. Once you find smoking unattractive, you will find no reason to smoke again.

Every behavior has two levels, one surface level is craving, and the other deeper level is motive. Our motives can be anything like, a motive to find true love and reproduce. A motive to find food and water. A motive to be socially accepted. A motive to reduce uncertainty.

Our habits are modern solutions to the former desires. Habits are like associations; these associations help us know whether we should repeat a habit or not. For example, if you notice that fire is burning, you will predict that if you touch the fire you will be burned, so you avoid touching it. Our behavior depends upon these predictions. These predictions are connected to our feelings, which then represent a craving.

A craving is a feeling which tells us that something is missing. When a habit describes a motive, you crave to do it again. You can make habits attractive if you associate them with positive feelings. In this way, you can make hard and tough habits attractive by linking them with positive events. You have to build this particular mindset, for example, many people find exercise very hard and challenging. So, instead of telling yourself that you need to do exercise every day, simply think that exercise will keep you healthy and strong. Change in attitude will help you develop your habit.

11

Walk Slowly, but Never Backward

T ry to use the Third Law of behavior change, make it easy. Try to make your habits easy to follow.

There are two types of behaviors. Actions and motions. An action is a type of behavior which leads you to a result or outcome. Motion is the type of behavior which does not directly lead you to the outcome. For example, If you find a diet plan and read some articles on it, that is motion, but if you eat a healthy diet, that's action.

So the question arises, why do we perform motion if it does not take us to our desired outcome? We actually do it for two reasons.

One reason for doing it is, it helps us in planning or learning. and secondly, it gives us the illusion that we are moving without failure. It is one of the main reasons why people avoid taking action because they don't want to take risks and face failure.

Therefore, they always stay in motion and delay taking action.

The key to master any habit is just practice, not perfection. You just need to do your daily tasks without any delay and the fear of failure. Just do it every single day. And eventually, you will master your habit. The best form of learning is the practice, not the planning.

Do you know how long it takes to form a new habit?

Habit formation is a process in which behaviors become automatic through repetitions. The more practice you do, the closer you are in making your habits automatic.

Neuroscientists call this concept: long-term potentiation. Long-term potentiation is nourishing the connections between neurons in the brain by repeating or patterning activities.

With the repetitions, cells improve their ability to send signals through neural connections.

Whenever you repeat any action, you are hitting specific neural circuit associated with that habit. Practice is the key to success. The more you repeat a habit, the easier it becomes to continue repeating that action.

12

The law of Least Effort

Human nature always follows the Law of Least Effort. This law explains that when we have an option to choose any one item between two similar things, we will always select the option that requires the minimum amount of work. We are easily motivated to do the least amount of work.

We need energy to do anything; similarly, we need energy to build any habit. If you require a high level of energy for a habit, soon you will become tired, and you will not succeed in developing your habit. For example, if you plan to do a hundred pushups a day. You will do it in the beginning because of your motivation, but soon you will be exhausted and stop doing them. But, if you do a single pushup every day, it will consume less energy and hence helps you in making it a habit.

There are many habits that you have developed using low energy. For example, checking your Facebook, listening to music, watching movies, eating junk food. These kinds of activities consume much of our time and are a quick dopamine fix.

We do not want to build habits; we just want immediate results. We do not want to make a habit of healthy eating and doing exercise, but we want to be super lean. We do not want to study seven days a week yet we want to have A grades. So if you wish to achieve your desired goals you have to cross the obstacle of building good habits.

The best way to overcome the obstacle of building good habits is by making them easier to perform. Make your habit easy to build and easy to follow.

We can easily build habits when it suits our lifestyle. Try to avoid or eliminate frictions in your habit formation. Eliminating friction from good habits will help you to perform them easily but adding friction into bad habits is good because it will help you to break them. Similarly, when we eliminate friction that consumes our time and energy, we can get more done with little effort.

13

How to stop procrastinating
Using Two Minute Rule

The main thing is not that you perform the actual habit, the important thing is that you just begin to act and move. Getting early at 6:30 in the morning, changing your gym clothes and sitting in the car is all evidence of a habit ritual. It shows that you will perform the exercise after getting to the gym.

The main thing is not about weight lifting but the routine of getting up and driving to the gym. The other thing is pretty apparent. Taking the first step of habit is difficult and that first moment will decide whatever happens in the next, either you will quit your habit ritual, or you are going to follow through. For example, if your routine is that when you come home from your job in the evening, you change into gym clothes and head straight towards the gym. So the moment you changed your gym clothes decided your next move. You can put on your workout clothes and go to the gym, or you can lay on the couch and watch movies.

41

Try to use two-minute rule. According to this rule, when you start a new habit, it should take less than two minutes to begin. It helps you to start your habit. For example, if you have to do thirty minutes of exercise, then it shouldn't take you more than two minutes to take out your exercise mat. Or, if you want to study, then you should be able to take out your notepad and books within two minutes. This is how you can cover your whole habit under two minutes. It acts as a starter. This idea helps you to make your habit easy to start and then you will end the activity by yourself.

Always remember a new habit should not be a challenge for you it should be easy to start. So you can continue doing it. Before you improve a habit, try to establish it. You will master any habit when you have the ability to do it regularly.

Two-minute rule is simply a psychological trick, you know you have to do more than two minutes of any habit but you initiate with a small and easy step. No one is going to do two minutes' workout, or read only one page of a book. But it does help you to start, the rest will follow automatically. You just need to make a ritual of starting up quickly and under two minutes.

14

How to make Good Habits Inevitable and Bad Habits Impossible

T he first step in making good habits inevitable and bad habits impossible is to use inversion of the third law of behavior change.

Make it difficult.

Try to make your bad habits difficult to follow. Use a commitment device to make your bad habits difficult.

A commitment device is an option you select in the present, but it controls your actions in the future. It helps you in building good habits and restrain you from bad ones. For example, if you want to control your over-eating habits, you can simply leave your purse or bank card at home while going out. In this way, you are not able to buy any food.

If you make your bad habit difficult or impossible you will break it. If you want to avoid checking your social media during work. Simply switch off your

43

phone and put it in another room while working. You have made it difficult for you to reach out to your phone, and you can study now without distractions.

You can use technology to automate your behavior it's a simple and effective way to ensure the right behavior and good habits. The things you can hand over to technology will save you time and help you to grow. For example, meal delivery services can do shopping for you. Website blocker helps to block social media browsing that wastes your productive time. Employees can save for retirement with automatic salary deduction etc.

15

Cardinal Rule of Behavior Change

The cardinal rule of behavior states that what is rewarded is repeated and what is punished is avoided. The feelings of pleasure tell our brain that the behavior is good, do it again. Positive emotions build your habits while negative emotions destroy them. The first three laws of behavior change are: make it obvious, make it attractive and make it easy, help to follow the behavior while the fourth law, make it satisfying helps to repeat the behavior.

That is how you complete a habit.

There are two types of environments. Immediate-return environment and delayed-return environment. In the immediate-return environment you are focused on the present and the very near future. You perform an act and it delivers an instant outcome. On the other hand, in the delayed-return environment, you do a job and wait for the reward at the end or late future. For example, you exercise today so that you could be in shape next year. We have embraced technology and times have changed, but the human brain did not evolve for life in the delayed-return environment. Therefore, we value present more than the future. Similarly, a reward which is received today feels better than a future reward.

If you perform a good habit, its reward is not immediate and is in the future, but if you perform a bad habit, it gives you an instant reward. Take the example of exercise versus smoking. If you do daily exercise, you will not get in shape instantly but can get results in the future. On the contrary, smoking gives you immediate stress reduction but harms you in the end.

It is not about awareness of this issue but actually bringing in consistency in your life.

If you want to keep a habit of doing good things you need to get immediate success or satisfaction, it will help you to stick with your habits.

16

How to Stick with Good Habits Everyday

The best way to stick with your good habits is with a Habit Tracker. One of the most satisfying thing in this world is seeing yourself progressing. You can use different visual measurement techniques to enhance your progress. For example, you can use paper clips, hairpins and marbles to measure your progress. If you are writing a book, then you can use this technique to improve your progress and satisfaction. Firstly make a target of writing specific page numbers then put that specific number of pins aside. Now place an empty jar on your table then start writing your book. Write one page and put a pin in the empty jar. It will give you instant satisfaction by achieving your target and help you in making progress.

A habit tracker is a simple solution to check and make records about your habits, whether you have performed your habits or not. For this purpose, the simplest method is to mark each productive day on your calendar. This is how you will get a record of your habit.

Many people use this technique to track their habits. The only thing you have to do is not to break the chain. If you are doing exercise then do not break the chain of doing it daily, you will get in shape faster. If you play and practice football daily, then do not break the chain and soon you will be champion in the team. Habit tracker is effective because it deals with multiple laws of behavior at the same time, such as making a behavior obvious, attractive and satisfying.

Habit tracking makes behavior obvious by creating a desire to act again. You get motivated because you see your progress and you do not want to break the progress chain. It gives you intense satisfaction to fulfill your habit. It also provides a visual record of your struggles.

Many people find it tough for them to do two things at a time, like doing the actual habit and then tracking it. You can make this task easy by immediately tracking your habit after doing it. When you complete your workout, go to your calendar and just mark it. Secondly, try to track one habit continuously instead of tracking ten habits.

Never break your chain of habit, if you do miss one day try to get back as soon as possible. Do not miss more than one day as it will break your chain of habit.

17

How an Accountability Partner Can Change Everything

Pain is a teacher. We repeat the behavior that is satisfying to us, but we do not repeat the experience with a painful ending. Similarly, when the failure is painful, we try to fix it, but when the failure is painless, we ignore it. You learn quickly from those mistakes that push you in critical situations. It is a common observation that the greater the damage, the faster people learn.

The best way to overcome bad behavior or bad habits is to link direct punishment with that behavior. For example, People pay their bills on time when you charge a late fee. Students attend their classes when you link the attendance with their grades. Punishment can only change the behavior when the strength of punishment is greater than the strength of bad behavior.

Laws and regulations in any country are also examples of habit contract. Seat belt law was first passed on 1st of December 1984 in New York. People did not wear seat belts at that time but after this law half of the nation started wearing the belt, because of the fine charges.

You can use habit contract to control your accountability. A habit contract is a verbal or written agreement in which you define your liability to any habit and the penalty that you have to face if you don't fulfill your liability. Now find two people who sign the contract with you, they act as your accountability partners.

You can also add an accountability partner to check whether you are performing your habit or not. We care deeply about what others think of us, and we do not want others to look down upon us. It is a great motivation if you know that others are watching.

18

Truth about Talent

I t is a simple truth that people are born with different skills and capabilities. Genes also play a role in this phenomenon. Genetics are useful in favorable conditions while they are useless in unfavorable conditions. For example, if you are a tall person. It's amazing for you to play basketball easily, but it's a difficult task to do gymnastics if you are seven feet tall. People that you see on the top of any field are not just trained, but they are the best suited for that job. It's like the right person in the right place.

To know which identity and habits are best for you is simply by understanding your personality. Know yourself first then figure out what is suitable for you. If you choose the right habit, you will succeed easily, but if you choose the wrong habit, then your life will become a struggle.

Picking a right habit means picking an easy habit and picking a wrong habit means picking a difficult habit. The best way to do this is by experimenting. There is a stage of exploring at the beginning of every task. Try to find a wide range of ideas and opportunities. When you win in any situation, explore it further. You can explore different options and then evaluate which one is suitable for you.

For example, you should explore different options and then evaluate that which work do you find enjoying yourself while others are complaining about it.

If you cannot win by being better, you can win by being different. You can combine your skills and reduce the competition. Try to master a specific skill it is called specialization, and it will increase your chance of success.

It would help if you focused on achieving your own potential rather than comparing yourself to others. Try to create and play the game that is in your favors.

19

The Goldilocks Rule

I t would be best if you always stayed motivated to work in life. Humans like challenges but only within a specific range, and by that I mean not too difficult. For example, if you want to play chess with a six years old child, you get bored easily, because it's too easy. However, if you play with Magnus Carlsen you will soon feel demotivated because the match is too difficult for you. But, if you play with someone who is of your caliber you will remain motivated. You have a chance of winning the game if you try hard.

This is what Goldilocks rule tells us. According to Goldilocks rule, you will get maximum motivation, when working on tasks that are neither too difficult nor too easy for you.

If you are starting any habit, try to keep it simple and easy to do. It will help you to stick with it easily. But, once a habit is developed then try to advance slowly and continuously. Without variety in life, you get bored easily. Boredom is one of the biggest hurdles in self-improvement.

Do you know how to stay focused when getting bored working on your goals?

How do you handle your boredom during your daily practice or training?

The difference between an average person and the successful person is that they find a way to show up at any cost. It's only normal that when you practice anything daily you will start losing your interest in it. So the easy solution is just to take a day off.

Do whatever you want to do but the next day start your practice again with a new surge of motivation.

Taking a day off will help you to refresh again. One of the greatest threats to success is boredom.

The difference between professionals and non-professionals is that they stick to their schedule no matter what happens in their lives. They never stop doing their practice or training even if they get bored.

20

The Downside of Creating Good Habits

Habits lead toward mastery. The more you practice any habit, the more you get efficiency and master it. The benefit of habits is that we do everything without thinking. However, the disadvantage is that we always do things in a specific manner and ignore small errors. You can achieve mastery by making a habit of deliberate practice.

Mastery = Habits + Deliberate Practice

In the process of mastery, you have to focus on small parts of success. By repeating one habit many times, it can make you achieve mastery in that habit. While doing your habit, you should pay attention to your performance. Your performance helps you to improve and enhance your ability. It tells you where you are making errors and where you need to change. You should make a system of thinking and

55

evaluating your performance. For example, if you play football every day, start making notes of your everyday practice. Then evaluate your performance and note down the areas that need to improve. In this way, you can improve your daily training and eventually you will achieve mastery.

Improvement is not merely about learning habits but it's more about thinking and evaluating your performance.

When you hold tightly to just one identity, it will make you fragile and easily breakable. Think about it, when you hold on to a single identity that defines you, you're easily breakable, because let's say that identity disappears tomorrow, then who are you at that moment? For example, when I was young I was an athlete and a baseball player, but after my accident, my baseball career ended, and I had to struggle very hard to find myself again.

Single identity makes it difficult for you to adapt to changes as well as challenges of life.

There is everything temporary in this world. Life is also continuously changing, so you need to pay attention to your old habits. Are they still useful to you? If not then you should replace them and create new useful habits that serve you.

CONCLUSION

Secrets to Results that Last

You cannot change your whole life by changing a single habit. In order to live a successful life, you have to change all your bad habits and replace them with good habits. You need to improve in all aspects of your life.

In the beginning, small improvements and changes seem meaningless, but over time you can see a whole new system created by you. Remember not to break the chain of making habits and improving. Throughout this book, I have mentioned four laws of behavior change. If you use these laws of making a habit obvious, making a habit easy, making a habit attractive and making it satisfying, these will help you throughout your life. And in the end, the secret to getting results that last is never to stop making progress and improving.

If you enjoyed this title, please consider leaving a review. Thanks